Vacation Ve

William M. MacKeracher

Alpha Editions

This edition published in 2024

ISBN : 9789362096609

Design and Setting By
Alpha Editions
www.alphaedis.com
Email - info@alphaedis.com

As per information held with us this book is in Public Domain.
This book is a reproduction of an important historical work. Alpha Editions uses the best technology to reproduce historical work in the same manner it was first published to preserve its original nature. Any marks or number seen are left intentionally to preserve its true form.

Contents

A WALK IN MOUNT ROYAL PARK: CANADIAN CITIES. ....- 1 -
STUDY IN SOLITUDE. ....- 3 -
IN THE SUGAR BUSH. ....- 4 -
IN MAY. ....- 8 -
THE BATTLE OF CHATEAUGUAY. ....- 9 -
EVENING IN JUNE. ....- 11 -
DEATH OF SIR JOHN. ....- 12 -
DOMINION DAY. ....- 13 -
RAIN FOR THE FARMER. ....- 14 -
COUNTRY BOY'S BOAST. ....- 16 -
BEFORE HARVEST. ....- 17 -
IN ANTICIPATION OF AUTUMN. ....- 18 -

A WALK IN MOUNT ROYAL PARK: CANADIAN CITIES.

Next morning in the Park I took a stroll.
   A walk upon Mount Royal is a thing,
Glorious at any time, but most of all
   At early morning in the opening spring,
   While yet the snow-wreaths to the rock-shelves cling,
And little streamlets lash the steaming side;
   While on the air the April breezes fling
An appetizing vigor far and wide,
And make the steep ascent a pleasure and a pride.

The path ascends by stately Ravenscrag,
   And past the monument which marks his rest,
Over whose history strange traditions drag
   Their spectral robes—his memory's sole behest.
   Here for a moment halting, all imprest
With other thoughts than find a ready tongue,
   I view the leopard slope, the bristling crest,
The blue beyond, with cloud veils lightly hung,
And glory in a dream of time when earth was young.

I follow by the winding road until,
   By taking at the sweep the northern arm,
I reach the summit. For the topmost hill
   The scenery reserves her chiefest charm;
   The upper sky is clear and light and warm;
The southern peaks that far away I wist,
   Seem close upon me; round their lower form
A shroud is wrapped; their tops, by sunlight kiss'd,
High in mid-air appear and mighty in the mist.

Beneath, the River spreads his glist'ning sheen,
   Spanned by not least of master workmanships,
Which sits as conscious daughter of a queen.
   And here art thou, my city, and thou dip'st
   Thy towers in the mist, whose magic strips
My spirit of the pall Time weaves—in vain;
   Nor Time nor Disappointment can eclipse
Days of young bliss—they must and will remain:
Once more a wonder thou, half city of the brain.

Fair art thou, City of St. Lawrence' Isle;
    Fair, City of the Hundred Spires; the seat
Of the Western Notre Dame, whose towered pile
    Rivals the first, of many a stately street
    And comely mansion, many a garden sweet,
Of Art and Nature, envious to please!—
    Thou of the mountain brow, before whose feet
The Northern Amazon his tribute fees,
Fraught with the waters of five mighty inland seas!

And fair art thou, whilome the Capital—
    Not what thou wert, but yet a gorgeous grave—
Fortress of fame, upon whose rocky wall
    Records of glory awe the trembling wave,
    Heights where the memories of heroes pave
The ancient streets and lustre all the scene!
    Fair, too, thou city where our fasces have
Their present rest; none worthier I ween!
And fair, ay, very fair, thou city called "Queen!"

STUDY IN SOLITUDE.

'Tis true, in midst of all, there may arise
    For man's society a sudden thirst,
A sense of hopeless vacancy which dries
    The spirit with a loneliness accurst,
    A longing irresistible to burst
The branchy brake with other birds to sing,
    Or, as, from where in solemn shades immerst,
The beetle comes to wanton on the wing
Around my lamplight flame—alas! poor, foolish thing.

But here thou may'st associate, though alone,
    With worthiest men, the best of every age,
Through whom the universe of thought has grown
    To what it is—the noble, good, and sage.
    How vain the fret, how frivolous the rage
For social rank, when thus e'en monarchs deign
    In close communion gladly to engage!
Nay, more than monarchs—Still the Mantuan swain
His fadeless laurel wears—What crowned Augustus' reign?

A thing of gold—'tis crumbled in the dust,
    The crowns of sovereigns and their sceptres all
Decay and are forgotten. Who would trust
    His fame to what fleet ruin must inthral?
    Tombs will obliterate and columns fall,
Annals be lost, and nothing have remained
    Of dynasties—The Conqueror of Gaul
And Lord of the World may yet have only reigned
By Shakspere's suff'rance—What hath all the rest attained?

IN THE SUGAR BUSH.

I halted at the margin of the wood,
    For tortuous was the path, and overhead
Low branches hung, and roots and fragments rude
    Of rock hindered the tardy foot. I led
    My timid horse, that started at our tread
And looked about on every side in fear,
    Until, arising from the jocund shed,
The voice of laughter broke upon our ear,
And through the chinks the light shone out as we drew near.

I tied the bridle rain about a tree,
    And on the ample flatness of a stone
Awhile I lay. 'Tis very sweet to be
    In social mirth's domain, unseen, alone,
    Sweet to make others' happiness one's own:
And he who views the dance from still recess,
    Or reads a love tale in a meadow, prone,
Secures the joy without the weariness.
And fills with love's delight, nor feels its sore distress.

This mind detained me in the night, but soon
    Far other thoughts usurped my regal soul,
With the Supreme made fitter to commune
    When human sympathy illumes the scroll
    And points the secrets of the mighty Whole.
I've spurned the earth to roam the Universe,
    And with the Eternal deadened Time's control,
For refuge from the shadow of a curse,
Or lust of curious lore—than maddest motive worse.

And Thou, Great Essence of all things that are,
    Hast been to me most prodigal of grace,
Thou'st smiled on me in many a twinkling star,
    The morn hath showered kisses on my face,
    In Nature's arms, thy bodily embrace,
Not purest poet hath more fondled been.
    'Tis true that I have often thought to trace,
Instead of peace, a harshness in thy mien,
And where I beauty sought, discordant sights obscene.

But not with aching heart I sought thee now,
    That thou might'st numb with thy narcotic night
The restless pulse, oblivious balm bestow,

    Infuse this frailty with thy glorious might,
        And blind with beauty to the mortal blight.
Not even wilful love possessed me, when,
        Behold, thy spirit stole upon my sight
And ravished me—What wonder that my ken
Forsook this little world of vanity and men?

And howsoe'er it seemed at other times
        To my imperfect and diseasèd mind,
Which darkened with the shadow of men's crimes
        Thy virtue, fancying in thee to find
        Reflection of the ills that shake mankind,
Though on me now a tempest broke and war
        Convulsed the elements, I would perceive behind,
Law, harmony, and purpose—That falling star
Seems sped to be the sun of new-formed worlds afar.

And yet the scene was such as often shares
        The obscurest soul—no wondrous rarity,—
The slender maples holding to the stars
        Their outstretched arms, as praying silently—
        A sea of stars—a dancing, dazzling sea,
Tremendous, mighty, infinite, supreme,
        Emblem of Might, Eternity's decree,
Half crediting the mythologic dream
And making of heaven th' abode that vulgar fancies deem.

A common scene, perchance, but, to the mind
        Which Nature hath enlightened with her ray
Nothing in her is common.—Not confined,
        Her beauty, to the sparkle and the play
        Of solitary spring, or rare bouquet
Of tropic flowers; she hath grandeur more
        Than crowns the mighty peaks of Himalay,
Or hurtles in the great Niagara's roar.
To me one beam of light can bring a priceless store.

Nay, more; the mind wherein her fulness dwells
        Can beauty and sublimity instil
In all created things, till it excels
        Even herself, though nurtured at her rill.
        The mind may be a monarch if it will,
And that of which great Nature is the nurse
        May rule itself, subjecting every ill,

And be the Sun, all phantoms to disperse,
And scatter glory round—Lord of the Universe.

What matter whether mortals own his sway?
   He knows his kingdom is not of this world;
It is within—perchance some purer day
   Will see the standard of his soul unfurled,
   When Good, surviving, sees the Evil hurled
To final dissolution, and the force
   Of worlds no longer round their centres whirled
Shall all combine and gather to the source,
To serve some nobler end—if such shall have recourse.

Rapt in the purple transport of a god,
   Pacing the ether with star-treading stride,
With conscious power, imperial purpose shod,
   And iris-crowned with radiating pride,
   I seemed to move—nay, move—what throbbing side,
Intenses immortality! what brow
   Thrills with severe conception!—deified,
As Pallas sprung.—Such did the gods allow—
I fear 'tis half a sin to tell what I do now.

If fire be stolen from Heaven, it is not
   The theft consigns the mortal to the shock
Of the Olympian vengeance; such the lot
   Of him whose earthly pride prepares the rock
   And taints the air where the penal vultures flock,
Whose after-weakness welds the fettering chain;
   Then gods despise and fellow mortals mock.
And here return me to the theme I've ta'en,
And sing the simple labors of the humble swain.

Their voices told they gave me welcome warm,
   Though oft their faces I can scarcely see,
For steam-clouds now atween us rise and swarm,
   And, rolling upward, find their vent in glee,
   Like more—alas!—too eager to be free,
Who fear to go, yet shudder to remain.
   Shall mortal spirits then be lost like ye?
'Tis ours, the burning heart, the boiling brain,
Which yield the vapor life.—But, then, ye fall in rain!

Ye fall in rain; ye change, but are not lost;
   Ye reach the ocean, and the mighty sea
Absorbs you in her bosom with the host

    Who have attested their eternity.
    And, if this world we quicken, so shall we,
When this dim, fluttering earthly scene is through,
    Commingle with the heroic and the free,
The pure, the good, the beautiful, the true,
Whose influence earth surrounds, and sheds its freshening dew.

*   *   *   *   *

I oped the door, supposing still 'twas night,
    But what a morn!—I seemed to half intrude
In sacred fane upon a holy rite;
    A purpled crimson peached the east, and strewed
    The whole horizon round with amethyst-hued,
Blue-bending tints. And as I forward rode,
    And in my hallowed east such vision viewed,
I thought of one o'er whom this glory glowed,
Who, like Aurora, soon would leave her soft abode.

IN MAY.

Now is the time when swallows twitter round,
    And robin redbreasts carol in the trees,
When the grass grows very green on lower ground,
    And opening buds embalm the buxom breeze,
    When orchards murmur with the half-blind bees,
Freed till th' uncellared hives again be full,
    The time when old men smile and maidens please,
Loose-zoned in summer dresses light and cool,
And laughing urchins shirk the lessons of the school.

Perchance it is the hour when dawn unveils
    The visage of the day; when o'er the bar
The radiant morning rides with saffron sails,
    Streamers of light on each resplendent spar,
    Fraught with rich gifts. Now, sunk, each faded star.
The Sun, the Sun,—the glorious Lord of Day!
    Behold, he comes! before his orbèd car,
Caparisoned with gold, in dazzling play,
Impatient dance his steeds to pace the purple way.

Or, is it in the cool and tranquil eve,
    When shadows lengthen and the shades increase,
When in the west celestial wonders weave
    Gorgeous Nirvanas of absorbent peace,—
    Transparency's impenetrable fleece,
Clouds of all colors floating every wise,
    On which the Sun looks up before he cease,
As some old man a moment ere he dies
Beholds with bliss serene the beauties of the skies.

THE BATTLE OF CHATEAUGUAY.

There is a valley where the wheat fields wave
   In autumn like a gold ymolten sea;
There is a river whose cool waters lave
   Sweet-scented gardens, groves, and rolling lea,
   And homes of people worthy to be free;
There is a name whose sound is like a song
   On lips of its own maidens—Chateauguay;
Yet mighty as the combat of the strong,
And glorious as the march of Freedom over Wrong.

And here they fought; and each encountered ten,
   With war-steed and artillery arrayed;
But righteous was their cause, and they were men,—
   Dark plumes of Iroquois, and Scotia's plaid,
   But most, the brothers of the arm which made
Napoleon terrible with triumphing.
   Between the foe and heaven they knelt and prayed,
Then, rising, heard their leader's summons ring—
"Such is our duty to our God—now for our King!"

Again they knelt; but now 'twas not to pray;
   A murd'rous volley crashes from their line;
But tenfold thunder mocks their mimic fray;
   From furious gun and flashing carabine,
   Like roaring billows and the driving brine,
The glut is backward hurled. Hurrah! 'tis vain!
   The vengeful fools, like men who war in wine,
Intoxicate with madness, overfain
For blood, have fired o'erhead, and not a man is slain.

Meantime, the valiant hero of the fight
   Upon his flank had foiled another foe,
Who now, retreating back in broken plight,
   Dismayed the rest with vision of their woe.—
   To see and seize, the leader is not slow;
He rushes to his buglers, bids them fast
   Withdraw into the woods, advance and blow—
"As for your lives this effort were the last!—
Yea, blow as Britain's throne depended on your blast!"

Away they ran, and, wheeling, sharply blew
   The wide-mouthed din obedient to his word:
Afar to north and south the echoes flew;

    The Indian child was startled, and the bird
        Affrighted from its peaceful nest; it stirred
The sluggish waters of the swart Outarde.
        Aghast, the Southron a great army heard,
And fled before the visionary sword,
As fled the Syrian host, deceived by Israel's Lord.

Back! cravens, back! in ignominy fly!
        Back to your homes, your country, and your slaves!
But thou art holy ground, and ne'er shall die
        Thy virtue and thy fame while still Time saves
        His best. And still shall states when conquest craves
From thee the salutary lesson learn,
        The poet call thy heroes from their graves,
To thee the warrior point, the patriot turn,
Thou last of Freedom's fields—Canadian Bannockburn!

EVENING IN JUNE.

The purple lilac with the dark green leaves
   A subtle perfume spreads o'er fields wherein
The meadow-lark with clear full singing cleaves
   The choral air. The rossignols begin
   A blither song, where the treacherous spiders spin
Their shimmering webs. The robin o'er her young
   Chirps cheerfully, or starts the frighted din.
Till the night oriole lights his lamp among
The blooms of marigold and spotted adder's tongue.

DEATH OF SIR JOHN.

What news to all alike brings startling sorrow?
   And he is dead, the vigorous chieftain dead?
Nor e'en for him would death still brook to-morrow?
   No more shall followers vaunt and foemen dread;
   No more by him the hot debate be led;
No more the lively tale, the clever jest
   Of him the State's most skilful, ablest head,
Albeit not her sternest, not her best,
But such is over now, then let his ashes rest.

When all was anarchy, he seized the reins,
   And broke and trained the fiery coursers young,
And from so many wide and fair domains
   One great Dominion 'neath his guidance sprung,
   Which he made glorious, till the nations rung
With our renown and his immortal name.
   But now his day was o'er; his work was done.
'Twas well.—He lived to hear his land's acclaim,
And perished in the pride of his Marengo fame.

Once more I see him—there once more he stands,
   Where midst the learned and beautiful he stood:
Scholars and knights, dames, statesmen clapped their hands;
   Within the glittering hall a thousand viewed;
   And ardent youth drank draughts to him imbrewed
With adulation. Run is glory's race.
   And this is Death,—that such a being should,
Who o'er his country soared in "pride of place,"
Be mingled with her dust like brutes and idlers base.

Softly, sweet River, softly by the cliff,
   Where in his eyrie the spent eagle sleeps!
Softly, beside where o'er one cold and stiff
   A hapless lady her pale vigil keeps!
   And come ye mourners—very heaven weeps—
With rue and rosemary from far and near,
   From Breton's capes and rude Columbia's steeps
To spread the shroud upon your hero's bier
While he who Laurel is will weave the cypress sere.

DOMINION DAY.

This is the day whereon, confederate
   In union, was our national'ty born,—
A four-walled temple beautiful and great,
   Arising like the bringer of the morn,
   Now winged and buttressed, which the years adorn
With pinnacles of fame. Long may it stand,
   Though realms be rent, states shattered, thrones uptorn!
Long may Canadians grasp each other's hand,
Defend their nation's rights, and love their fatherland!

RAIN FOR THE FARMER.

If gently falls the small, soft, lazy rain,
    To indoor industries he shrewdly steals;
And in the barn from some neglected grain
      The choking chaff the clattering fanner reels;
    Or in the shed the sapling ash he peels
For handles for the fork with humor blithe,
    Or haply lards the tumbril's heavy wheels,
Or of the harness oils the leather lithe,
Or turns the tuneless stone and grinds the gleaming scythe.

But now the sky is black; and now the Storm
    Prepares his legions for the coming fray,
While murmurs low prelude the dread alarm,
      As prayed the hosts,—like robèd monks who pray
      Mid slumb'rous incense in a cloister gray,—
Till from yon cloud the fiery signal given
    Enrages all their terrible array.
Jove's flaming car is o'er Olympus driven,
And thunders roll along the threshing floors of heaven.

Hark to the rolling of the sulphurous sea,
    Upon its shores its billows beat amain;
In angry tumult, furious to be free,
    It rends the cloud with one tremendous strain;
    The chasm is closed!—once more!—again in vain!
Again! again! Each time, enraged to yield,
    It hurls its threats in throes of Titan pain;
While crouch the cattle 'neath their oak-tree shield
And horses, frantic-eyed, in terror hoof the field.

The screaming birds, low-flying, seek their nests,
    The swaying sport of panic and the gale,
The tall trees, trembling, bend their creaking crests;
      The ramping engine shrieks upon the rail—
      How helpless all things seem! how poor, how frail!
Until the welkin warfare's awful knell
    Is voice of all below in piteous wail.
Alas! for him who toils in Erie's swell,
And for the timid soul which loveth life too well!

Still roars the thunder, still the skies are rent
    With frenzied flame,—the swift electric chain,
Jerked clanging backward when its charge is spent.

    Such overhead; but now upon the plain
        There is a lull, a listening for the rain.
The air grows still; she feels 'twill not be long;
        Like to a poet when o'er heart and brain
The stern, relentless tyranny of Wrong
In knolling tumult broods.—He knows 'twill break in song

And now at last it comes, crashing and cool
        And sweet; well for the earth and what is sowed!
Well for the harvest! See, it fills the pool,
        In little streams goes leaping down the road.
        And now the winds are joyous, and they goad
Their fallen foe, until he half repeats
        His former fury.—One might think it snowed.
And sweep from the roofs like dust from driven streets,
The spirits of the storm, wrapt in their winding-sheets.

COUNTRY BOY'S BOAST.

And hath he not whereof he needs must sing?
    And hath he not whereof he well may boast?—
He from whose kin so many a one did spring
    To shape the mighty rocks that guard the coast
    Of History 'gainst Time, lest all be lost;
And chiefly those who stamped the speaking page,
    Who bore the standard of Achievement's host
In Fame's tenth legion, from the earliest age
Till stately Vergil wrote, till Chelsea's Vulcan sage.

Judea's royal, world-renowned bard
    Was once a shepherd. How must Bethlehem's hills
Have leaped and grown more lovely as they heard;
    Till raging monsters, music-charmed, he kills.
    And saves his flock, or with his harping stills
More dire destroyers in his monarch's breast!
    And whence did Job arise, that prince whose ills,—
Lost, flocks, lands, family, all that he possessed,—
Wrung the immoral song his virtue to attest?

Let him be proud in later days to roam
    In Warwick vales by virtuous Avon's shore,
Through fields of Ayr, around the humble home
    Of him, the Cincinnatus of song, or o'er
    Ettrick and Tweeddale in their days of yore,
Or with the *Seasons'* bard on Cheviot green,
    With young Chile Harold laugh o'er Loch na Garr,
The Solitary trace through Cumbrian scene,
Or weep on Sussex downs with him of gentle mien.

BEFORE HARVEST.

And now 'tis time for Harvest. Hark! and lo,
   With ringing sound of full melodious horn,
Over yon eastern hill-top all aglow,—
   Her sickle gleaming in the golden morn,
   Her arm upraised with sheaf of yellow corn,—
She comes elate with light, elastic pace;
   Her neck and zone full-clustered vines adorn;
Her saffron locks, fruit-crowned; her luscious grace;
Her round and ripened form; her fair, benignant face.

And now the fields, when suns serenely greet,
   A rich and mellow, wanton joy afford:
The russet pease vines, and the burnished wheat
   And whiter barley,—hating to be stored,
   Guarding with jealous spears their precious hoard,—
The tapering oat-stalk, dangling beads of gold:
   In brilliant sea of beauty all outpoured,
With dazzling depth of splendor all untold,
Where fleets of zephyrs skip in fold that follows fold

Like to a dream I had but yesternight,
   Of pure, transporting, childlike playfulness,
The presence of a fair-haired, blue-eyed, bright,
   Thoughtless and laughing.—Words can not express
   In *poet* phrase the fulness that did bless
Entrancingly my vision. I advanced
   Behind to worship. Straight each golden tress
Was ruffled and about my face they danced,
Smoth'ring with beauty, while the maiden gleeful glanced.

IN ANTICIPATION OF AUTUMN.

But now the Summer hastens to its close,
    And soon will Song a different aspect wear,
Sweeping terrific, clad in ghostly snows,
    And lit by the flash of the Boreal glare,
    Or, but a poet in his easy chair;
And her most pleasing aspect now beguiles
    What time is hers with deft, endearing air:
With gorgeous gold she decks her garments, whiles
Her melancholy face with Indian Summer smiles.

Thy very smile sends sadness to my heart.
    Farewell! sweet love, the happy hour is o'er:
Too well I knew that we again must part.
    Her garments trail the fond, reluctant floor.
    But I shall ne'er forget the dress she wore,
Her looks, her words, the pleasing song she sung—
    'Tis melody will charm me more and more,
'Tis music that will keep my spirit young,
'Tis joyance in my soul, though jarring on my tongue.

I've hummed the music after thee as well
    As changing tones of youth allowed, and fear,
And vexing sprites that choke the upward swell.
    But yet, perchance, some bosom it may cheer,
    By recollection making thee more dear
To those who've drunk thy music at its spring,
    To some, mayhap, who never learned to hear,—
Alas! poor, wretched souls!—its sound may bring
Some semblance of thy strain, some wish to hear thee sing.

What though I have expounded nothing new,
    And traced, I trow, unworthily the old?
Song is no mystic science.—Men may do
    Strange things in other spheres, and may unfold
    Secrets unthought, tell tales before untold;
But what thou wilt, the bard; nor less, nor more.
    And to the mind informed in Nature's mould
Thou has revealed thyself—the same of yore,
The same to-day thou art, and shalt be evermore.

Let them who will, content themselves to sing
    In trifling pageantry and gilt array,
To pluck the song-beads from the shimmering string

  That skirts thy robe. But such my soul doth sway
  As makes me hang upon thy breast and say
"*I love thee!*"—as a mistress?—then mine own;
  Blindly and recklessly?—some future day,
Mine eye, from thine clearer and stronger grown,
May thrid the straggling stars and search the deepening dawn.

O, make my soul an argosy of song,
  Tranquilly floating on a sea of peace,
As with her rowers beautiful and strong
  Some trireme bears among the Isles of Greece
  With music-muffled oars! Give safe release
From murky moorings, storms, and rocks that jar,
  And let its pearls in purity increase,
Until with singing sails it cross the bar
To melt in golden waves with gems of many a star!